Knowsley Library Service

Please return this book on or
before the date shown below

Knowsley SLS
Project Loan

FISH

PREDATORS

Written by
Mignonne Gunasekara

BookLife
PUBLISHING

©2020
BookLife Publishing Ltd.
King's Lynn
Norfolk PE30 4LS

ISBN: 978-1-83927-260-8

Written by:
Mignonne Gunasekara

Edited by:
Shalini Vallepur

Designed by:
Amy Li

A catalogue record for this book is available from the British Library.

CONTENTS

Words that look like <u>this</u> can be found in the glossary on page 24.

MEET THE PREDATORS

Welcome to the world of predators. Predators are animals that hunt other animals for food. They come in many shapes and sizes, but they all have something in common — to their <u>prey</u>, they are terrifying!

Habitats are the homes in which animals, plants and other living things live.

In this book, we will be looking at predators that are fish. They rule their underwater habitats with their weapons and strength.

GREAT WHITE SHARK

Powerful tail

Great whites have around 300 teeth that are arranged in rows.

Sharp teeth

The great white shark is the largest predator on Earth that is a fish. It can grow to be six metres long and has a strong <u>sense</u> of smell.

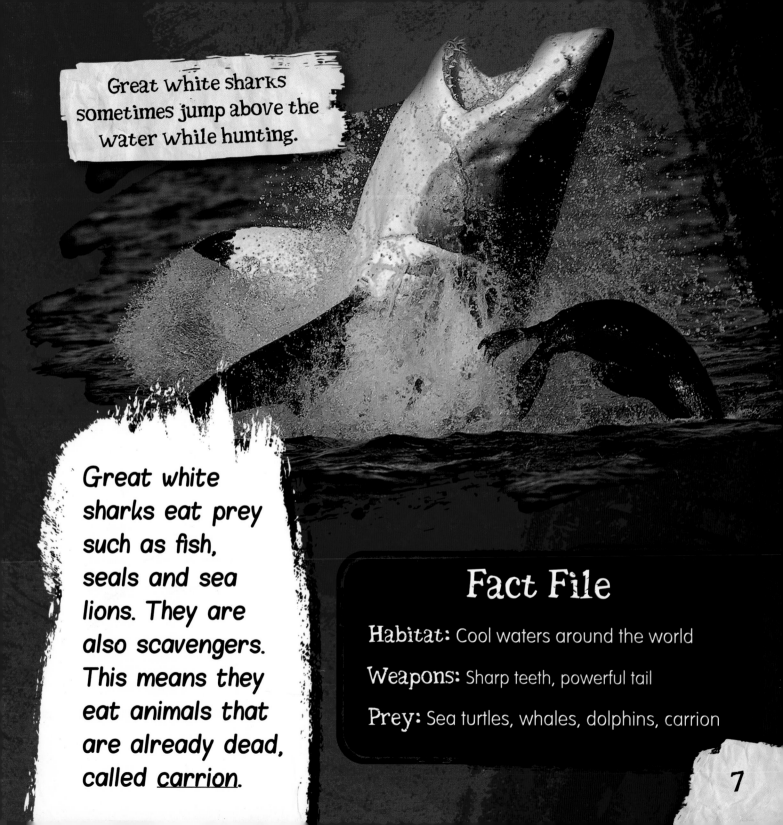

Great white sharks sometimes jump above the water while hunting.

Great white sharks eat prey such as fish, seals and sea lions. They are also scavengers. This means they eat animals that are already dead, called _carrion_.

Fact File

Habitat: Cool waters around the world

Weapons: Sharp teeth, powerful tail

Prey: Sea turtles, whales, dolphins, carrion

7

STRIPED ANGLERFISH

Striped anglerfish can be found in many different habitats, such as by rocky and coral <u>reefs</u>. They are usually about ten centimetres long but can grow to be 25 centimetres long.

Striped anglerfish use <u>camouflage</u> to hide from both predators and prey.

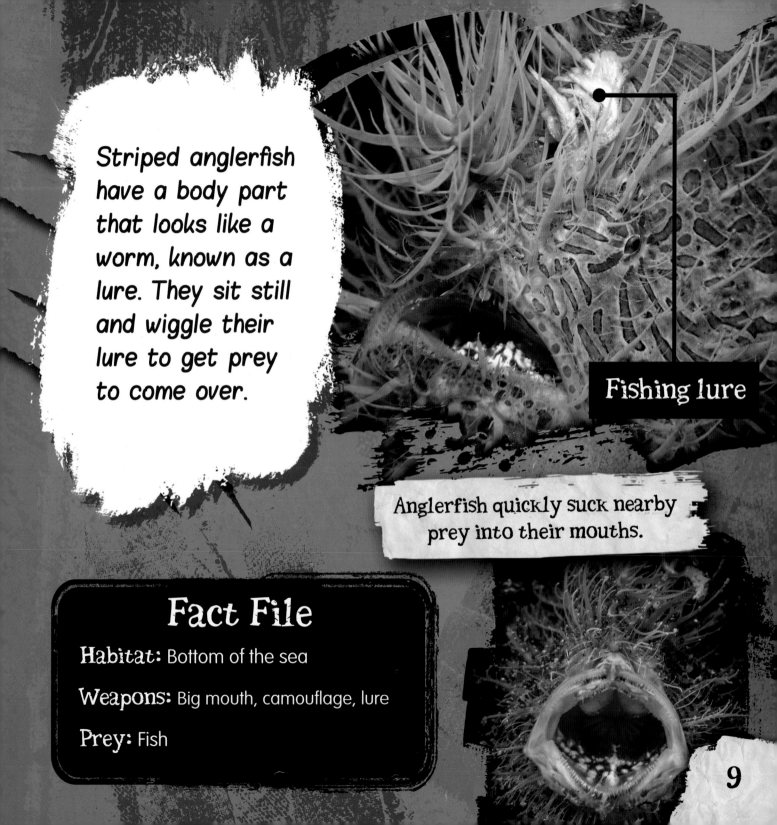

Striped anglerfish have a body part that looks like a worm, known as a lure. They sit still and wiggle their lure to get prey to come over.

Fishing lure

Anglerfish quickly suck nearby prey into their mouths.

Fact File

Habitat: Bottom of the sea

Weapons: Big mouth, camouflage, lure

Prey: Fish

GREAT BARRACUDA

Sharp teeth

Adult great barracudas usually live alone.

Great barracudas have very long bodies and can grow to be two metres long. The bottom part of a great barracuda's mouth sticks out farther than the top part.

Great barracudas hunt by surprising their prey. They swim at prey really quickly and snap them up in their large mouths.

The great barracuda eats fish such as anchovies.

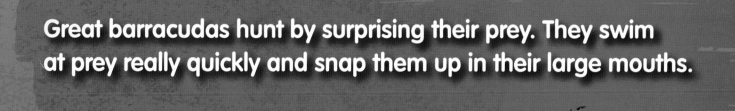

Fact File

Habitat: Warm waters around the world

Weapons: Speed, sharp teeth

Prey: Smaller fish

11

BLOTCHED SNAKEHEAD

Blotched snakeheads are very interesting because they are fish that can breathe air. This means they can stay out of the water for quite a long time.

Most fish can't breathe when they're out of the water.

Blotched snakeheads live in waters with plenty of plants to hide behind.

Blotched snakeheads are ambush predators. This means they hunt by surprising prey that come near them, rather than chasing after prey.

Fact File

Habitat: Waters in Africa and Asia

Weapons: Camouflage, surprise attacks

Prey: Fish, frogs

13

RED LIONFISH

Red lionfish can be found in the Indian Ocean, Pacific Ocean and Atlantic Ocean. Their long, colourful fins have <u>venomous</u> spines that help protect them from predators.

Spines

Red lionfish stings can be very painful.

Long fins

Red lionfish are ambush predators. Some have been seen backing prey into a corner by stretching out their fins. The prey is then quickly snapped up to eat.

Fact File

Habitat: Rocky and coral reefs

Weapons: Venomous spines

Prey: Fish, shrimp

Red lionfish swallow their prey whole.

ELECTRIC EEL

Electric eels can make enough electricity to hurt a horse – or a person!

Electric eels can make <u>electricity</u> in their bodies. They use it to <u>stun</u> prey while hunting and to scare predators away.

Electric eels can't see very well – they use electricity to work out where to go.

Electric eels come up to the top of the water to breathe air through their mouths.

Fact File

Habitat: <u>Fresh water</u> in South America

Weapons: Electricity

Prey: Fish, <u>crustaceans</u>, <u>amphibians</u>

17

RED-BELLIED PIRANHA

Red-bellied piranhas can grow to be just over 30 centimetres long.

Sharp teeth

Red-bellied piranhas have sharp, triangular teeth. They also have an amazing sense of hearing and can hear prey splashing around from far away.

Red-bellied piranhas are scavengers. This means they eat what they can find and don't always kill their own prey. Sometimes, they will even eat plants.

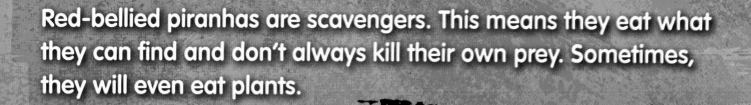

Piranhas will swim towards the smell of blood in the water.

Fact File

Habitat: South American rivers and lakes

Weapons: Sharp teeth, good sense of hearing

Prey: Fish, insects, worms

REEF STONEFISH

Reef stonefish are the most venomous fish in the world. They have spines in their fins that can push venom into anything that attacks them.

Reef stonefish go as deep as 20 metres underwater.

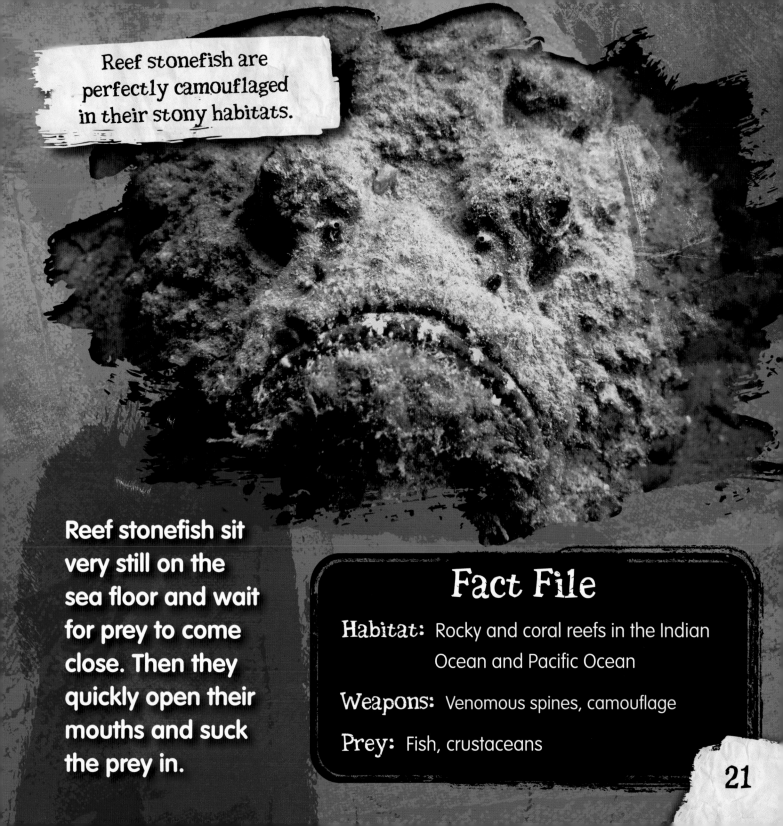

Reef stonefish are perfectly camouflaged in their stony habitats.

Reef stonefish sit very still on the sea floor and wait for prey to come close. Then they quickly open their mouths and suck the prey in.

Fact File

Habitat: Rocky and coral reefs in the Indian Ocean and Pacific Ocean

Weapons: Venomous spines, camouflage

Prey: Fish, crustaceans

GROW FOR IT

Congratulations, you met the predators! Weren't they fierce? Let's see how big these fish can get!

Reef stonefish

40 centimetres

Great white shark

600 centimetres

Great barracuda

38 centimetres

Red lionfish

25 centimetres

200 centimetres

Striped anglerfish

Which fish grows to be the longest?

GLOSSARY

amphibians	animals that can live both on land and in water
camouflage	things about an animal that allow it to hide itself in a habitat
carrion	rotting parts of dead animals
crustaceans	animals that live in water and have a hard outer shell
electricity	a powerful type of energy that can cause a painful shock
fresh water	water that is not salty
prey	animals that are hunted by other animals for food
reefs	rocky places underneath the sea where many creatures live
sense	a way for the body to get information about the world; can be touch, taste, smell, hearing or sight
stun	make an animal pass out using a blow or shock
venomous	able to poison another animal through a bite or a scratch

INDEX

Photo Credits. All images courtesy of Shutterstock. With thanks to Getty Images, Thinkstock Photo and iStockphoto.

Recurring images – Ameena Matcha (old paper), teacept (header font), Alexey Pushkin (grunge texture), MrNoe (claw marks), Olga_C, Ografica (grunge shapes). Cover – ARTYuSTUDIO, Damsea, p2–3 – ARTYuSTUDIO, p4–5 – Jennifer Mellon Photos, Volodymyr Burdiak, p6–7 – Sergey Uryadnikov, Jennifer Mellon Photos, p8–9 – Sascha Janson, John A. Anderson, p10–11 – New Media and Films, Shane Gross, p12–13 – underworld, Grigorii Pisotsckii, p14–15 – underworld, Grigorii Pisotsckii, p16–17 – Bigone, tristan tan, p18–19 – FormosanFish, p20–21 – Kristina Vackova, Vladimir Wrangel, p22–23 – Fotokon, kaschibo, New Media and Films, Palomba, Vladimir Wrangel